I0475217

Table of Contents

Foreword

JAMES THOMSON, Partner, Buy Box Experts

This is the complete Amazon Solution Providers Directory for sellers. It is intended to help all retailers solve the Rubik's cube that is the Amazon marketplace. We are here to demystify it, allowing you to use Amazon as a weapon in your distribution and revenue growth arsenal -- rather than viewing the marketplace as competition.

Produced by BigCommerce and the founders of the Prosper Show, James Thomson and Joseph Hansen, the Amazon Sellers' Solution Provider Directory has been a year in the making. Within, you'll find more than 230 companies offering some of the most successful seller services available to alleviate pain points associated with selling on Amazon.

These are the solutions and seller services used by the highest-grossing companies incorporating Amazon as part of their channel strategy. Each of these solutions will save you time, optimize your operations and ultimately work to increase revenue made from the Amazon marketplace.

The directory is organized by vendor category to help you easily find the software, tools and services most relevant to your business. In each section, you will find tips concerning when your company should begin to engage with these solutions as well as a few key issues to consider.

Eliminating the steep learning curve associated with Amazon selling success will enable you to grow your sales and prepare your business for the future of commerce.

01 Amazon Product Research: Tools, Software, & Sourcing

Amazon Product Sourcing: Where Do Your Competitors Get Their Products?

As you research potential manufacturing partners for your private label business, you can access public import records to see from where your competitors are sourcing their products. Think of this as a shortcut to identifying overseas manufacturing capabilities similar to what you need.

Key Issues to Consider

Just because your competitors are using specific overseas manufacturers doesn't mean you will be able to get cooperation from the manufacturers to make your products. Keep in mind; these manufacturers may not be able to accommodate your custom design needs. It is a good place to start, however, without having to make a whirlwind trip overseas to identify suitable manufacturers.

Company	URL	Email
Import Genius	www.importgenius.com	info@importgenius.com
Panjiva	www.panjiva.com	contact@panjiva.com

Amazon Price Tracker

Realistically, you should install these free tools immediately upon becoming an Amazon seller. By being able to determine listing activity across other sellers on listings you currently have or are considering adding to your catalog, you can gauge likely types of pricing competition you will face. You will also be able to understand whether the product has been sold by Amazon itself.

KEY ISSUES TO CONSIDER
Remember, it's critical to look at historical pricing information so you aren't getting a static and potentially misleading picture of competition. For example, you may see the product you're aspiring to sell has very little competition only to discover a week later that Amazon itself is selling this product. It was only temporarily out of stock, at which point you will be back to competing head-to-head with Amazon. This is something that may cause you to rethink whether you want to sell that item.

Company	URL	Email
Camel Camel Camel	www.camelcamelcamel.com	support@camelcamelcamel.com
Keepa	www.keepa.com	info@keepa.com

Inventory Scouter

If part of your sourcing model includes retail arbitrage, you can save yourself a lot of time by having one of these tools accessible when you walk the aisles of your retail sources. By scanning barcodes to produce instantaneous Amazon product and profitability information, you can quickly establish whether an item makes sense to buy for resale on Amazon.

KEY ISSUES TO CONSIDER
Most of these tools look only at Amazon fees and your cost of goods sold. You should

factor in any indirect and overhead costs into your decision on whether to buy any of these items for resale. In doing so, you may find that some of the estimated profitable items you've scanned aren't profitable and that your time wandering the aisles inspecting product isn't, in fact, free. There is real opportunity cost to your time.

Company	URL	Email
ASellerTool	www.asellertool.com	support@asellertool.com
Neatoscan	www.neatoscan.com	info@neatoscan.com
Profit Bandit By Seller Engine	www.sellerengine.com	sales@sellerengine.com
Scan Power	www.scanpower.com	support@scanpower.com
Scout Pal	www.scoutpal.com	support@scoutpal.com

Amazon Product Research

When you go looking for new products to add to your Amazon catalog, you may find yourself scouring through supplier catalogs or staring at spec sheets. Just how are you making your decisions about what to add?

Are you able to screen hundreds and thousands of prospective products on criteria like Amazon customer demand, Amazon seller competition, the presence of Amazon Retail as one of the competing sellers, margin opportunity, and so on? Without some automated tools, you likely aren't able to do a deep-dive on most prospective products.

Fortunately, these product research tools can help accelerate this evaluation process significantly, allowing you to become more efficient and data-driven in your sourcing decisions.

KEY ISSUES TO CONSIDER

While the line between inventory scouter software and product research software is closing every day, I typically see more types of data in the product research software. But, you have to figure out how to incorporate these additional data points into your decision on whether to source specific items.

Also, keep in mind that product attractiveness can change very quickly by the introduction of a just one lower-cost competitor, so make a habit of revisiting this information on a regular basis.

Company	URL	Email
AMZShark	www. amzshark.com	hello@amzshark.com
ASIN Tool	www. asintool.com	support@asintool.com
EcomSpy by Ecom Engine (FBA Spy)	www.ecomengine.com	n/a
Etail Insights	www.etailinsights.com	n/a
FBA Toolkit	www.pathfinding.com.ar	contact@pathfinding.com.ar
GetAMASuite	amasuite.thgwebmedia.com	n/a
INDBL	indbl.com	n/a
Jungle Scout	www. junglescout.com	support@junglescout.com
Novel Rank	www. novelrank.com	admin@novelrank.com
Sales Rank Express	salesrankexpress.com	n/a
Scope by Seller Labs	sellerlabs.com	n/a
Seller Metrics	sellermetrics.com	n/a
Sellerstoolbox	sellerstoolbox.com	n/a
Sellics	www. sellics.com	info@sellics.com
TeraPeak	www.terapeak.com	n/a
Wiser	www. wiser.com	info@wiser.com
AMZ Secrets	amzsecrets.com	n/a

Company	URL	Email
AMZInsight	www.amzinsight.com	n/a
ZonGuru	zonguru.com	n/a
amazooka	www.amazooka.com	n/a
AMZ Tracker	www.amztracker.com	n/a
AMZ One	www. amz.one	info@amz.one
AMZ Space	amz.space	n/a
Manage by Status	managebystats.com	n/a
Unicorn Smasher	unicornsmasher.com	n/a
Launch List Formular	www. launchlistformula.com	members@launchlistformula.com
Launchzon	www. launchzon.com	promo@launchzon.com
Jump Send	jumpsend.com	n/a
Ama Specialist	www. amaspecialist.it	info@amaspecialist.it

02 Amazon Product Listing Optimization

Product Photo Editing & Cleanup

Even the best product photographer's photos may need some cropping, whitening or general adjustment to get the image in line with Amazon requirements.

This cleanup can take a lot of time when considering the addition of dozens or hundreds of new listings. This is not an ideal way for you to invest your time in your business. Fortunately, these low-cost, quick-turnaround options are available, allowing you to take moderately professional photos and get them cleaned up for primetime on Amazon.

KEY ISSUES TO CONSIDER
Only so much cleanup can be done on a bad photo. It's ideal to get some feedback on a test run of photos you take to make sure you have provided these companies with an adequate quality of photo before modification.

Company	URL	Email
Clipping Magic	www.clippingmagic.com	support@clippingmagic.com
Pic Monkey	www.picmonkey.com	n/a
Pixelz	www.pixelz.com	n/a

Amazon SEO: Keyword Research

Whether you are looking to optimize new listings or existing listings onto which you have added your product offers, it's important to understand what keywords Amazon customers are using to find your product. Otherwise, you may have a fantastic product that never gets discovered by Amazon customers or loses out on suitable keyword traffic.

KEY ISSUES TO CONSIDER

Customer preferences can change over time, meaning that your keyword selections today may need to be updated later. Consider refreshing your primary listings at least annually. Also, remember that customers may be finding your products through keywords that aren't obvious to you today. There is a significant benefit in referencing the large historical databases that these providers have built to match keywords with products.

Company	URL	Email
AMZ Tracker (Unicorn Smasher)	www.amztracker.com	n/a
Keyword Inspector	keywordinspector.zendesk.com	support@keywordinspector.zendesk.com
Keyword Tool Dominator	www.keywordtooldominator.com	n/a
Keywords Suggestion	n/a	n/a
Merchant Words	contact@merchantwords.com	contact@merchantwords.com
SearchRank by Seller Labs	searchrank.sellerlabs.com	n/a

UPC Barcodes – Purchase

If you are building a private label business on Amazon, you're going to need UPCs (Universal Product Codes) for each product you list. We also want to mention that you should not be buying UPCs to put onto other companies' existing products. We have seen too many new listings get created that are duplicates of existing listings, but the new seller didn't do the necessary work of matching its offers to the existing listings in the Amazon catalog.

KEY ISSUES TO CONSIDER
Never recycle UPCs onto other products. Once a UPC has entered Amazon's catalog, it is tied to a specific item. If you decide to stop carrying one private label product, don't use that UPC for some new item. You will create a mess for yourself that can result in hundreds of canceled or returned orders and far too much negative feedback.

Company	URL	Email
Instant UPC Codes	www.instantupccodes.com	n/a
Speedy Barcodes	speedybarcodes.com	n/a
UPC Barcodes	www.pixelz.com	info@upcbarcodes.com

Amazon Data Management & Feed Integration

As you increase the number of new listings in your catalog or you consider adding new marketplaces (beyond Amazon) to your overall business, it will quickly get very complicated to keep track of all the columns of data needed for your listings (whether on Amazon or other marketplaces). By working with a company that specializes in keeping up with what columns of data are needed in each category of each marketplace, you can save yourself a lot of time building and maintaining your product feeds.

KEY ISSUES TO CONSIDER
Some inventory and order management solution providers indicate that they offer listings functionality in their tools. But first, you need to be sure your product categories on your desired marketplaces are all covered by your inventory/order management solution provider. Some companies pick an apparent "all-in-one" inventory/order management partner only to discover not all listing templates needed are available. This requires the seller to work with a data feed provider anyway.

It is also worth mentioning that if your business is all-Amazon, and focused exclusively on adding offers to existing listings that someone has created, your need for a data feed provider is going to be low, as you aren't likely contributing new data or editing existing data on your listings.

Company	URL	Email
Aten Software	www.atensoftware.com	n/a
CommerceHub (Mercent)	www.picmonkey.com	support@mercent.com
Datafeedwatch	www.pixelz.com	support@datafeedwatch.com
Go Data Feed	www. godatafeed.com	contact@godatafeed.com
Goat Consulting	www.goatconsulting.com	n/a
Listtee	www. listtee.com	help@listtee.com
NChannel	www.nchannel.com	n/a
Salsify	www. salsify.com	info@salsify.com

Get Amazon Product Reviews

If you sell private label product, you should be immediately looking for ways to get legitimate product reviews on your items from the get-go. The presence of a minimum 5-10 product reviews per private label product helps to reduce a customer's hesitancy to purchase, as the customer can read what others have written about your product. Furthermore, listings with product reviews are much more likely to get better search results on Amazon than products with no sales history.

KEY ISSUES TO CONSIDER

There are unfortunately a few sites that offer illegitimate product reviews where the reviewer has never seen the product, and writes product reviews blindly for cash. After recent crackdowns at Amazon on such reviews, there are much more strict rules about how product reviews need to be sourced, and Amazon is now watching more carefully than ever before to make sure reviews are legitimate.

"Verified purchase" reviews are much more valuable than reviews that haven't come from "verified" purchases, raising the importance of not only getting product reviews on new listings, but also getting some initial sales on those items which will then lead to "verified" product reviews. Most of the solution providers mentioned here will help you get sales on your new products, coupled with verified purchase product reviews. This is a powerful duo for new product launches.

Company	URL	Email
Amazon Reviewer Network	www.amazonreviewernetwork.com	n/a
AMZ Tracker, Amazon Review Club	www.amztracker.com	n/a
Bqool	www.bqool.com	n/a
Flashbuz	www.flashbuz.com	info@flashbuz.com
GiveAwayService	www.giveawayservice.com	n/a
Ilovetoreview.com	www.ilovetoreview.com	info@ilovetoreview.com
Product Elf	www.productelf.com	n/a
Product Rocket	www.productrocket.io	n/a
Review Kick	www.reviewkick.com	support@reviewkick.com
Sales Backer	www.salesbacker.com	n/a
Snag Shout by Seller Labs	www.snagshout.com	n/a
Tomoson	www.tomoson.com	n/a
Viral Launch	www.viral-launch.com	service@viral-launch.com
Zonblast	www.zonblast.com	n/a
Reviewbox	www.getreviewbox.com	info@getreviewbox.com

Get Amazon Feedback

Feedback is one of the critical measures used by Amazon to evaluate sellers, while also providing prospective customers with guidance on how efficiently you have historically provided high-quality product on time to other Amazon customers. From the first Amazon sale you make, Amazon tracks how you are doing both in terms of average feedback as well as overall feedback count. Your feedback score will be used in evaluating if you qualify for the Buy Box.

Ideally you should aim for an average feedback score above 98%, while below 90% is likely to result in a loss of your Buy Box privileges. In fact, for brand new sellers (not using FBA), it is common for you to have to wait at least a month building up the number of feedback before Amazon will allow you to become "Buy Box eligible." Feedback matters from day one on Amazon, and you need to collect feedback from your customers.

KEY ISSUES TO CONSIDER

Many sellers choose to manually solicit customers directly for feedback through Seller Support. While that is allowed according to Amazon's Terms of Service, the process can get rather unscalable as your business grows. Fortunately, there are software providers that can make this feedback request process an automated process, complete with easy-to-use templates.

Company	URL	Email
Feedback by Bqool	www.bqool.com	support@bqool.com
Feedback Five By Ecom Engine	www.feedbackfive.com	info@feedbackfive.com
Feedback Genius By Seller Labs	www.sellerlabs.com	n/a
FeedbackExpress	www.feedbackexpress.com	n/a
Feedbackz	www.feedbackz.com	help@feedbackz.com
Kibly	n/a	n/a
Mr Feedback	www.mrfeedback.com	n/a

Company	URL	Email
Reseller Ratings	www.resellerratings.com	n/a
Sales Backer	www.salesbacker.com	n/a
Jump Send	www. jumpsend.com	n/a

Re-Pricing Tools & Services

If you are competing head-to-head with other sellers on your listings, it's likely you are fighting it out over price. As other sellers reduce prices, your product becomes less interesting and less visible to customers as a result of losing the Buy Box. That is, unless you can reduce your price too, ensuring your ability to remain competitive for the Amazon Buy Box. As you know, products that appear in the Amazon Buy Box sell 4x more than those that don't ever make it in, and an estimated 90% of new product sales come from products in the Buy Box.

KEY ISSUES TO CONSIDER
When you sign up for a re-pricing tool, you will need to identify your floor price for each item. To do that effectively, it is best to have a strong grasp of your all-in costs by SKU (including indirect and overhead costs). That way, you aren't inadvertently setting a floor price that is underwater for you, all in the name of getting the sale at all cost. Let's focus on remaining profitable.

Also, keep in mind that pricing alone does not determine if you will win the Buy Box. Without strong performance metrics across the board (related to customer service, late shipment rate, cancellation rate, negative feedback, etc.), your ability to match your competitor on price and get your fair share of the Buy Box will be hampered significantly. Next, remember that not all of your competitors are equal, even if their prices are equal. Keep an eye out for Amazon Retail offers and FBA seller offers. With those in place, it will be harder to use a re-pricer to match price alone and get your fair share of the Buy Box.

The list below includes standalone re-pricing tools. It's worth noting that many of the inventory management and order management solution providers offer integrated re-pricing tools as part of their software.

Company	URL	Email
Appeagle	www.appeagle.com	info@appeagle.com
Bqool	www.bqool.com	n/a
Channelmax	www.ecatalogservices.com	sales@ecatalogservices.com
Feedvisor	www.feedvisor.com	info@feedvisor.com
Logicsale	www.logicsale.en	service@logicsale.en
Mean Pricer	www.meanrepricer.com	n/a
Repriceit	www.repriceit.com	n/a
Repricer Express	www.repricerexpress.com	n/a
Seller Vision Pro	www.sellervisionpro.com	info@sellervisionpro.com
Sellery by Seller Engine	www.sellerengine.com	sales@sellerengine.com
Smart Price by Ecom Engine	www.ecomengine.com	n/a
Teikametrics	www.teikametrics.com	info@teikametrics.com
Wiser	www.wiser.com	info@wiser.com

Translation Services

If you are looking to expand your business into other marketplaces, you may need to get your listings data translated. In most Amazon marketplaces, the listings must be in-language for the local country.

KEY ISSUES TO CONSIDER

While free tools like Google Translate are useful for simple translation of common phrases, they are not yet anywhere near the level of accuracy to capture marketing nuance or technical product explanations that are common in product descriptions, bullet points and titles.

Company	URL	Email
Akorbi	www.akorbi.com	n/a
Intercultural Elements	www.intercultural-elements.eu	info@intercultural-elements.eu
Jonckers	www.jonckers.com	n/a
JR Language	www.jrlanguage.com	info@jrlanguage.com
Lionbridge	ondemand.lionbridge.com	n/a
Straker Translations	www.strakertranslations.com	n/a
Translations.com	www.translations.com	n/a
Web Interpret	www.webinterpret.com	sales@webinterpret.com
Interpro Translation Solutions	www.interproinc.com	n/a
geekspeak	www.geekspeakcommerce.com	services@geekspeakcommerce.com
Gengo	www.gengo.com	sales-us@gengo.com
Moravia	www.moravia.com	n/a
SDL Managed Translation	www.sdl.com	n/a
TextMaster	www.textmaster.com	sales@textmaster.com
Transn	www.transn.com	amz@transn.com
Youdao	service.netease.com	fanyi-service@service.netease.com

Split Testing Tools

For the more sophisticated seller, a new tool has recently become available to help sellers test out different versions of product images, content and pricing.

This tool is useful specifically for the seller that controls the listing content of specific products. In such situations, it makes a lot of sense to see how customers respond to different content.

We like the experimental, scientific nature of such a tool, and encourage you trial out a variety of these tools. We hope to see many more tools available to help sellers to test and refine what they are doing, just as Amazon does itself today with thousands of daily tests on its website.

KEY ISSUES TO CONSIDER
Sellers should be open-minded that customers may surprisingly respond to content that isn't the Sellers' own favorite content. So it's up to sellers using this software to test a wide range to evaluate relative effectiveness of such content. Furthermore, testing should not be done along a "1 and done" approach, but rather regular testing and improving on listings (much like how Amazon constantly evolves through its nonstop testing efforts).

Company	URL	Email
Splitly	www.splitly.com	n/a

03 Amazon Inventory, Orders & Warehousing Directory

Inventory & Order Management

If you are a multi-channel seller, keeping track of your overall inventory levels can get tricky. If you oversell inventory, you upset customers and are on the fast track to getting your Amazon account suspended. And if you undersell, you have lost out on sales. You need to have real-time inventory numbers to manage inventory by channel, giving you the ability to replenish FBA quickly (if required) or place new product orders with your suppliers if you are running out on critical selection.

KEY ISSUES TO CONSIDER

There is quite a bit of variation across inventory and order management companies. Some charge a percentage of sales, while others charge by the number of orders processed. Some incorporate sophisticated analytics and purchase order management tools, while others incorporate some listing functionality, repricers, accounting software integration and shipping rate optimization tools. Also, not all marketplaces can be handled by each inventory and order management tool today. Careful due diligence on such centrally critical software is necessary for the individual business owner.

Ask each company:
- What's included and what's not?
- How much automation of which steps can the software do?
- How much flexibility do you have to roll into or out of the software? How long is the on-boarding process, and what "house-in-order" steps are required of you to get started?

Company	URL	Email
BalanceMaxx	www. ecatalogservices.com	sales@ecatalogservices.com
Brightpearl	www.brightpearl.com	n/a
Browntape	www.browntape.com	contact@browntape.com
Ecomdash	www.ecomdash.com	support@ecomdash.com
Etailsolutions	www.etailsolutions.com	info@etailsolutions.com
Fillz	www.fillz.com	sales@fillz.com
Getcarta	www.getcarta.com	info@getcarta.com
Linnworks	www.linnsystems.com	info@linnsystems.com
Monsoon Commerce	www.monsooncommerce.com	n/a
Orderhive	www.orderhive.com	support@orderhive.com
Ordoro	www.ordoro.com	info@ordoro.com
Retailops	info@retailops.com	info@retailops.com
Salesdash	www.salesdash.com	n/a
SalesWarp	www.saleswarp.com	sales@saleswarp.com
Selleractive	www.selleractive.com	support@selleractive.com

Company	URL	Email
Sellercloud	www.sellercloud.com	info@sellercloud.com
Sellerexpress	www.sellerexpress.com	n/a
Skubana	www.skubana.com	info@skubana.com
Solid Commerce	www.solidcommerce.com	contact@solidcommerce.com
Stitchlabs	www.stitchlabs.com	support@stitchlabs.com
Volo	www.volocommerce.com	n/a

Multichannel Selling Solutions

For a seller looking to build and house its listing data in one place, as well as to coordinate inventory across multiple marketplaces, the multichannel sales providers offer a suitable solution.

KEY ISSUES TO CONSIDER

While the combined use of a listing solution and an inventory and order management solution may be appropriate for some sellers, other sellers solve the listing-inventory-order issue using a single solution. For sellers using this second option, the companies below offer support to multi-channel sellers, getting their listings and inventory organized and pushed out to various sales channels.

Company	URL	Email
Channel Advisor	www.channeladvisor.com	n/a
Channel Unity	www.channelunity.com	n/a
M2E Pro	n/a	n/a
Retail Tower	www.retailtower.com	n/a
Sellbrite	www.sellbrite.com	n/a
SureDone	www.suredone.com	n/a

Shipping Services & Providers

While many Amazon sellers are 100% FBA sellers, using Amazon's UPS Ground program for inbound shipping to Amazon's fulfillment centers, anything beyond that model will require shopping for shipping solutions.

KEY ISSUES TO CONSIDER

Many Amazon sellers are 100% FBA sellers and use Amazon's UPS Ground program for inbound shipping to Amazon's fulfillment centers. If you want to use anything beyond that, it will require shopping for shipping solutions.

Company	URL	Email
Endicia	www.endicia.com	n/a
Ordoro	www.ordoro.com	info@ordoro.com
Parcel Hub	www.parcelhub.co.uk	n/a
ShipperHQ	www.shipperhq.com	sales@shipperhq.com
ShipStation	www.shipstation.com	n/a
Shipworks	shipworks.com	n/a
Trulycommerce	www.trulycommerce.com	info@trulycommerce.com
Deliv.Co	www.deliv.co	n/a
Postmates	www.postmates.com	support@postmates.com
Shyp	www.shyp.com	biz@shyp.com
Stamps.Com	www.stamps.com	n/a
Shippo	goshippo.com	n/a
Ordercup	www.ordercup.com	info@ordercup.com

Company	URL	Email
Shiphero	www.shiphero.com	hello@shiphero.com
Shiplark	www.shiplark.com	n/a
ShippingEasy	www.shippingeasy.com	n/a
Shiprobot	www.shiprobot.com	n/a
Shiprush	www.zfirmllc.com	info@zfirmllc.com
Teapplix	www.teapplix.com	n/a
Trueship	www.trueship.com	n/a
4PX	4px.com	n/a
AGLC	n/a	contact-us-zexp@amazon.com
Aramex	www.aramex.com	vernon.martin@aramex.com
Bombino	www.bombinoexp.com	Uttam@bombinoexp.com
CK1	www.chukou1.com	contact@chukou1.com
CNE Express	www.cneglobal.net	info@cneglobal.net
EDA	www.edayun.cn	business@edayun.cn
Encompass Shipping	www.encship.com	info@encship.com
oPostg	www.epostg.com	customersupport@epostg.com
First Choice Shipping	www.firstchoiceship.com	support@firstchoiceship.com
Logistics Plus	www.logisticsplus.net	amazonretailer@logisticsplus.net

Company	URL	Email
Nippon Express	www.nittsu.com	NEUSSPCC@nittsu.com
Pantos	www.pantos.com	sangbum.lee@pantos.com
Spainbox	www.spainbox.com	n/a
Transglobal Express GmbH	www.transglobalexpress.co.uk	amazon@transglobalexpress.co.uk
Woodland Group	www.woodlandmedia.com	paul@woodlandmedia.com
ZHY	zhykg.com	sima@zhykg.com
B2C Europe	n/a	sales@b2ceurope.eu
SFC Service	n/a	NEUSSPCC@nittsu.com
WNDirect	n/a	amazon@wndirect.com

Third-Party Logistics (3PL)

Do you pride yourself on moving into bigger warehouses every couple of years, all because your business keeps growing? Are you spending more and more of your time managing your warehouse (staff, equipment, operations), rather than building your business? You probably didn't become an entrepreneur to become an expert on the intricacies of managing a warehouse.

KEY ISSUES TO CONSIDER
While competitively-priced 3PLs can be more expensive than the out-of-pocket costs of running your own warehouse, your most precious asset is your time to spend on building your business. Be prepared to spend a little more on warehousing through a 3PL in order to free yourself up from all of the headaches a warehouse often brings a small business owner.

Not all 3PLs are equally experienced at FBA prep, poly bagging, bundling and kitting. Do your research carefully, and talk with case study clients that the 3PL provides. Also, expect some transition period up front as you train the 3PL employees on exactly the process you want for your order processing.

Company	URL	Email
Newgistics	www.newgistics.com	contact@newgistics.com
Pnpline	www.pnpline.com	cs@pnpline.com
Prep It Pack It Ship It	www.PrepItPackItShipIt.com	west@PrepItPackItShipIt.com
Prep Label Box	n/a	preplabelbox@yahoo.com
Prime Zero Prerp	www.primezeroprep.com	n/a
SellTecPrep	www.SelltecPREP.com	Info@SelltecPREP.com
SM Operators	www.smoperators.com	sales@smoperators.com
Swan Packaging Fulfillment	www.swanpackaging.com	tim@swanpackaging.com
Transtrade	www.transtrade.com	experts@transtrade.com
Storefeeder	www.StoreFeeder.com	Hello@StoreFeeder.com
Ukfulfilment.co.uk	www.ukfulfilment.co.uk	n/a
Wiseloads	wiseloads.com	n/a

04 Returns, Accounting & More Post-Sales Services

Return Management & Reverse Logistics Services

As the number of orders increases, so too will your number of returns. Those returns can be rather annoying to manage and often include the inspection, grading and testing, upgrading, repackaging, etc.

Given that customers rarely send back all of the product, warranty, instruction manual and packaging, there is likely to be additional work needed to attempt to convert a returned item to a re sellable item (hopefully in "new" form again).

If you have more than one full-time employee working just on returns, it's time to be asking questions to these solution providers to see if they can streamline this headache for you.

KEY ISSUES TO CONSIDER
Returns can cost you money in return fees and repackaging, but they also cost a disproportionate amount of time to repair versus selling a unit newly sourced from your

supplier. There is a size-able opportunity cost to managing returns, both in terms of time, and potentially the lack of expertise on how to maximize recovery rates on those returns. These solution providers know the in's and out's on how to make the returns process less painful and costly for you.

Company	URL	Email
Tradeport	www.tradeportusa.com	info@tradeport.com
Genco Marketplace	www.GencoMarketplace.com	support@GencoMarketplace.com
Newgistics	www.newgistics.com	contact@newgistics.com
OpenedBoxReturns.com	www.openedboxreturns.com	info@openedboxreturns.com
Optoro	www.optoro.com	inquiries@optoro.com
Rebound Returns Management	www.tsbsupplychain.com	info@tsbsupplychain.com
4PX	www.4px.com	n/a
CK1	www. chukou1.com	contact@chukou1.com
EDA	www. edayun.cn	business@edayun.cn
Ezi Returns	www.ezireturns.com	info@ezireturns.com

Accounting

Every company needs to keep track of its financial position, including expenses such as payroll and insurance, purchase orders, inventory value and margins. The following software programs are commonly used by online sellers to track these numbers.

KEY ISSUES TO CONSIDER
While Amazon is not known for providing sales and revenue data that can be easily incorporated into accounting software, some of the companies below have developed API and conversion tools to absorb existing Amazon data into their tools. Further simplify your life by looking for accounting software that integrates into Amazon's Seller Central.

Company	URL	Email
Quickbooks	www.intuit.com	n/a
Sage	www.sage.com	n/a
Wave Apps	www.waveapps.com	n/a
Xero	www.xero.com	sales@xero.com

Accounting and Bookkeeping Support

Long before you have a mountain of shoeboxes full of receipts, it is important to be tracking all of your income and costs. This way, you can maintain a macro view of your financial position at any given moment, rather than waiting until year-end when taxes are due.

Face it; almost no one likes recording all of their financial data, but it's necessary to know where you are doing well and where improvements are immediately needed. Rather than put unnecessary lags between paperwork coming in and you understanding how that paperwork reflects your true financial position, these solution providers offer you the ability to keep an eye on your financials without having to deal with the laborious task of sporadic, manual data entry.

KEY ISSUES TO CONSIDER

These companies can offer basic book-keeping, or full-scale accounting (including income tax preparation and inventory reconciliation support). Depending on how complex your inventory and channels are, you may want to outsource more and more of this to focus on your skills sourcing profitable product.

Company	URL	Email
Bench.co	www.bench.co	help@bench.co
Catching Clouds	www.catchingclouds.net	info@catchingclouds.net
TechFinance	www.techfinancecfo.com	n/a
KPMG	www.kpmg.com	n/a

Company	URL	Email
Meridian	www.meridianglobalservices.com	help@bench.co
Pitney Bowes	www.dutycalculator.com	support@dutycalculator.com

Tax Calculation and Remittance

In which states do you owe sales tax? Are you collecting enough sales tax in enough states?

If you can't answer these questions today, it's time to look for support. And if you can answer these questions, and you're required to pay in more than 2-3 states each quarter, you probably could benefit from the streamlined processes these companies will be able to provide you. No more manually filing papers to each required state. These companies will streamline all of that for you, and keep on top of ever-changing tax rules for each tax jurisdiction (state, county, city, etc.) in which you have tax nexus.

KEY ISSUES TO CONSIDER

Whether you collect state tax or not on your online sales, you almost certainly are liable for paying the state taxes. Work with your tax attorney to confirm where you owe state taxes, and then consider using Amazon's tax collection services to streamline the collection process, while using any of these solution providers to support the tax remittance process.

Company	URL	Email
Avalara / Trustfile	www.avalara.com	n/a
Taxify	www.taxify.co	n/a
TaxJar	www.taxjar.com	support@taxjar.com
Vertex	www.vertexSMB.com	info@vertexSMB.com
Meridian Global Services	www.meridianglobalservices.us	n/a

Profitability Analysis

If you understand your all-in-costs by SKU, you can figure out your profitability by SKU, which will guide your actions on inventory management, vendor negotiations, sourcing of new products and pricing. If you keep your total sales revenue and total gross margin each aggregated, then you have no visibility on specific product issues or opportunities which ultimately drive your overall profitability. Most sellers realize they need more granular profitability analysis when they experience YOY sales growth that is not matched by at least the same growth in YOY gross margins.

KEY ISSUES TO CONSIDER

Rarely do all products in a seller's catalog generate positive margins, once consideration for indirect and overhead costs are made. Only at the point that all costs have been allocated down to the individual SKU level can a seller take immediate necessary action to course correct on product selection.

Please note that many of the inventory and order management tools have incorporated profitability analysis tools into their overall structure. These companies below are stand-alone applications.

Company	URL	Email
Amazonworks	amazoworks@amazoworks.com	amazoworks@amazoworks.com
Sales Calc	www.salecalc.com	n/a
Daily Source Tools	www.dailysourcetools.com	james@dailysourcetools.com
Hello Profit	www.helloprofit.com	help@helloprofit.com
Fetcher	www.fetcher.com	n/a

Cash Management Tools / Financing Options

Most entrepreneurs think they need more capital. Depending on how well organized your accounting books are, there are plenty of organizations that will lend various amounts of money to build up your businesses.

KEY ISSUES TO CONSIDER

Being an Amazon seller can be risky if you're not paying attention to the road all the time. Bringing lenders into the equation adds more risk – risk that can be well managed if you are properly managing your overall business.

If you don't know what you are doing as an Amazon seller, it's probably best not to get too involved in using some else's money.

As an FBA seller, you won't be able to grant "first lien" rights to most lenders, as Amazon doesn't allow anyone into their fulfillment centers to take control of inventory used as collateral in a loan. So be prepared to get very little funding based purely on the value of FBA inventory – other assets are required typically.

Company	URL	Email
Payability	www.payability.com	support@payability.com

05 Amazon Customer Management Solutions

Amazon Account Management Consultants & Services

Selling on Amazon is difficult, even for the largest, more experienced sellers on Amazon. To stay on top of best practices and make sure that those longer-term "back burner" projects get properly addressed, it is sometimes necessary to bring in an account management consultant. These consultants can provide short-term or medium-term support. Given that an account management consultant is working typically with multiple sellers, this person will have seen a lot of behaviors – good and bad – that can be used as benchmarks to give you a richer perspective of where you can improve. The consultant is also likely to provide a valuable perspective, removed from your heavily invested day-to-day view of everything you are doing to run your business today.

KEY ISSUES TO CONSIDER
With no certification needed to become an Amazon consultant, anyone could declare him or herself as such, resulting in a wide range of skills and capabilities. It is critical for sellers to do due diligence and authenticate the quality and expertise of a consultant. Every seller

should start with the assumption that there are no silver bullets to being a successful seller on Amazon. It takes operational discipline and relevant data to do this well, so look for consultants who can help with operations and data.

Company	URL	Email
All Industry Consulting	www.allindustryconsulting.com	steve@allindustryconsulting.com
Amazon Consulting Experts	n/a	n/a
Buybox Experts	www.buyboxexperts.com	info@buyboxexperts.com
CPC Strategy	www.cpcstrategy.com	contact@cpcstrategy.com
Deniz Olmez	n/a	olmezd@gmail.com
Digital Brand Works	www.digitalbrandworks.com	hello@digitalbrandworks.com
Elemerce	www.elemerce.com	ty@elemerce.com
Evolved Commerce	www.evolvedcommerce.com	matt@evolvedcommerce.com
FitForCommerce	www.fitforcommerce.com	info@fitforcommerce.com
Lance Petit Consulting	www.lancepettit.com	n/a
Lisa Suttora Ecommerce Marketing Strategies	www.whatdoisell.com	lisa@whatdoisell.com
Marketplace Ignition	www.marketplaceignition.com	info@marketplaceignition.com
Simple Sales Solutions	www.simplysalessolutions.com	kelly@simplysalessolutions.com
Velocity Marketing	www.velocity-mktg.com	lance@velocity-mktg.com
Vostok Partners	www.vostokpartners.com	n/a

Company	URL	Email
Whitebox.co	www.whitebox.co	support@whitebox.co
Zanoma	www.zanoma.com	n/a

Cross-Border Currency Management

If you are selling product on an international Amazon marketplace, you are paying Amazon upward of 3.5%-4.0% transaction fee to handle currency exchange and wiring of your funds back to the U.S. That sort of hidden fee is size-able on otherwise low-margin products. Fortunately, these solution providers streamline the process for you. With them, you can cut that cost in half and recapture margin you didn't realize you were losing.

KEY ISSUES TO CONSIDER

These solution providers can streamline the process because they set up foreign bank accounts for you. Those bank accounts require a bunch of paperwork. Prepare to invest several hours reviewing legal paperwork to get set up in each foreign country. Once you are setup, you are good to go.

Company	URL	Email
Currencies Direct	n/a	n/a
Payoneer	payoneer.custhelp.com	n/a
Worldfirst	www.worldfirst.com	enquiries@worldfirst.com

Automate Messaging

Unless you plan on signing into your Seller Central account every 24 hours of every day of the year, you leave yourself exposed to the possibility that a new inquiry from a customer goes unanswered within the required 24 hour period. These solution providers help to meet Amazon's requirement of a 24-hour timeframe for responding to Amazon customers, while letting you enjoy your weekend or brief holiday.

KEY ISSUES TO CONSIDER

Many of these automated messaging services send customers a generic response. You should still plan to provide the customer a more expansive response within a couple of business days, as customers want their questions properly answered before buying your product or filing negative feedback.

Company	URL	Email
Fusion By Xsellco	www.xsellco.com	info@xsellco.com
Reply Manager	www.replymanager.com	info@replymanager.com
ChannelReply	www.channelreply.com	n/a

Customer Email Support

What happens when you are starting getting dozens of customer emails a day, asking the same types of questions over and over? Each email must be answered quickly and accurately so as to keep the customer happy. If you're looking to streamline the process of answering these emails, good customer email support software will help to semi-automate your responses. The same way that Amazon's Seller Support has created standard responses for certain commonly asked questions, these software programs can help you streamline answers to your most common customer inquiries.

KEY ISSUES TO CONSIDER

Most multi-channel sellers find that the level of customer emails they get from Amazon customers is far lower than other marketplaces. Often the questions will be related to some sort of shipping-related issue. If a seller is predominantly using FBA for its Amazon catalog, it's likely such software won't be needed for the Amazon portion of the seller's overall business.

Company	URL	Email
Desk.com	www.desk.com	sales@desk.com
Freshdesk	www.freshdesk.com	support@freshdesk.com

Company	URL	Email
Helpscout	www.helpscout.net	n/a
Zendesk	www.zendesk.com	support@zendesk.com

Minimum Advertised Price (MAP) Violation Monitoring

This software is usually relevant only for brand owners, rather than resellers, as it is the brand owner that wants to identify MAP-violating resellers. If you are a private label manufacturer or brand owner supplying Amazon resellers with product that is supposed to be sold at MAP levels, these software packages can provide you with accurate, real-time data on which sellers are violating MAP. This allows you to have a data-driven discussion with specific resellers about these issues.

KEY ISSUES TO CONSIDER
Amazon doesn't monitor MAP levels on products for brand owners. It's up to the brand owner to do this him or herself, and work with his or her own distribution channels to address these issues.

Company	URL	Email
Channel IQ	www.channeliq.com	n/a
Competera	www.competera.net	info@competera.net
Itelligence	www.iTelligence.com	support@iTelligence.com
Marketplace Repricing	www.marketplacerepricing.com	sales@marketplacerepricing.com
Newmo	www.newmo.com	n/a
Oris Intel	www.orisintel.com	n/a
Price Grid	www.pricegrid.com	sales@pricegrid.com
Price Manager	www.pricemanager.com	info@pricemanager.com

Company	URL	Email
Price Spectre	www.pricespectre.com	n/a
Profitero	www.profitero.com	sales@profitero.com
Teikametrics	www.teikametrics.com	info@teikametrics.com
Upstream Commerce	www.upstreamcommerce.com	sales@upstreamcommerce.com
Wisemapper By Wiser	www.wiser.com	info@wiser.com

Virtual Assistants

If you are spending far too much time on trainable, repetitive or administrative tasks that someone else could handle, consider getting yourself a virtual assistant for additional support. Maybe it's setting up phone calls with your suppliers, answering emails, basic book-keeping or reporting generation work that you need to regularly do, but find you don't have enough time to stay on top of such tasks. With the development of a whole industry of skilled, English-speaking assistants, you can free yourself up to work on the highest-value activities.

KEY ISSUES TO CONSIDER

No one ever does work as well as you do! Well actually, that may not always be true, but it does take time to get comfortable delegating responsibilities to someone else, especially someone based remotely. With technologies like Skype, instant messaging and phone available, it takes only a little discipline to remain in regular communication with your assistant. You will likely find that your virtual assistant is better organized on the tasks you assign to him/her, as they have fewer tasks.

If you go down the path of using a virtual assistant, keep in mind that you need to keep these people motivated and feeling valued. Read a book like "Virtual Freedom" by Chris Ducker to get yourself up to speed on what it realistically takes to get set up in an effective virtual assistant relationship.

Company	URL	Email
247virtualassistants.com	www.247virtualassistants.com	n/a
Hire My Mom	www.hiremymom.com	n/a
longerdays.com	www.longerdays.com	n/a
mytasker.com	www.mytasker.com	info@mytasker.com
Time Etc	web.timeetc.com	n/a
uassist.me	www.uassist.me	info@uassist.me
Virtual Staff Finder	www.virtualstafffinder.com	n/a
virtualemployee.com	www.virtualemployee.com	n/a
Zirtual	www.zirtual.com	sales@zirtual.com

06 The Best Marketing Services for Amazon Sellers

Sponsored Product Ads Tools

After recent changes in the product review rules at Amazon, many more sellers are becoming focused on advertising to drive traffic to their products.

While the Sponsored Product ad offering by Amazon provides sellers with opportunities to increase traffic to their listings, competition for the limited ad space is quickly increasing.

Sellers need to become much more sophisticated in their bidding strategies and available budgets. Fortunately, new software is available to help sellers make sense of the return on investment of the endless number of keywords that could be used to promote individual products through Sponsored Products.

KEY ISSUES TO CONSIDER
Customer search behavior changes over time, so it's ideal to continue using such tools on a regular basis, constantly improving the effectiveness of advertising efforts. Words

and terms that are not effective today may become more effective in a few months, as customers are exposed to new product choices.

Company	URL	Email
PPC Scope	www.ppcscope.com	support@ppcscope.com
SellerLift	www.sellerlift.com	amazon@sellerlift.com
Ignite from SellerLabs	www.sellerlabs.com	support@sellerlabs.com

Landing Pages

Common situations you'd need a landing page for include:
- You are building a shopping site using your own domain
- You are creating a temporary flash site

In both situations, you probably don't want to waste a bunch of time figuring out how to get your site operational and looking decent for customers. Fortunately, these providers offer you easy-to-use, inexpensive tools so you can focus on selling, rather than becoming a frustrated web designer.

KEY ISSUES TO CONSIDER
Speed vs. bell-and-whistles functionality is the major tradeoff. While you may need a more permanent site, the tools of these providers are meant to get you up and running quickly. If you want much more advanced functionality, it will take time and likely the help of a web designer to get the perfect look and feel for your long-term site.

Company	URL	Email
Launchrock	www.launchrock.com	n/a
Prefinery	www.prefinery.com	n/a

Logo Design

If you are building your own website or your own brand, you will likely want to build a logo for these assets. And you most likely aren't as artistic as you are entrepreneurial, so look at these solution providers. Some offer a single design, while others use a competitive approach to getting you many options from which to pick your preferred.

KEY ISSUES TO CONSIDER
Some of these sites allow you to enforce an NDA with your designers, so as not to publicize pre-launch that your website or product is coming. Be sure to give your designers information on what the website or product is meant to do and the audience it is targeted toward.

Company	URL	Email
48 Hours Logo	www.48hourslogo.com	n/a
99 Designs	www.99designs.com	n/a
Crowdsite	www.crowdsite.com	n/a
Design Contest	www.designcontest.com	n/a
Design Crowd	www.designcrowd.com	n/a
Design Hill	www.designhill.com	n/a

Social Media & SEO

If you have your own site or brand, it can be beneficial to bring in an expert – even for just a few months – to build exposure of your assets quickly, with the careful expertise of someone who does this sort of thing over and over. They can provide bandwidth creating new marketing content that is used to spread the word on your product, or they can manage the distribution of any existing content you already have.

KEY ISSUES TO CONSIDER
While no directory could possibly include all of the skilled social media marketing people out there, here are a few to get you started. There are many skilled people in this space, so

if you are looking at improving awareness in a local area, ask other companies who might have had direct experience with local providers.

Company	URL	Email
Big Leap	www.bigleap.com	n/a
Foxwell Digital	www.foxwelldigital.com	n/a
Micro Media Marketing	www.micromediamarketing.com	n/a
Rumor Advertising	www.rumoradvertising.com	n/a
SEO National	www.seonational.com	n/a
Boonze Media Solutions	www.boonze.com	amazon@boonze.com

Task Outsourcing

Let's face it, you don't have enough time to get everything done! There is a whole world of talented freelancers out there that can handle all sorts of projects for you.

If you're running short on time or expertise to complete specific types of tasks, these companies organize freelancers to make it easier for you to find people who will help. Freelancer services range and include: consulting, designing, writing, creating listings, improving marketing materials, building websites or software, handling repetitive data look-up tasks, etc. Chances are some other Amazon sellers have already defined Amazon-seller tasks for these freelancers. It's worth exploring what talented help might be out there to support your business today.

KEY ISSUES TO CONSIDER
Some tasks may involve sharing confidential or semi-confidential information, so be careful about what you choose to outsource. Check to see that your work is being done by the person you're talking with on these sites. Sometimes work gets farmed out, and you don't know who's doing the work. Interview multiple people and give them small test projects to see if you have good communication and work well together on getting expected results back within the expected timeframe.

Company	URL	Email
Freelancer	www.freelancer.com	n/a
Upwork	www.upwork.com	n/a
Fiverr	www.fiverr.com	n/a